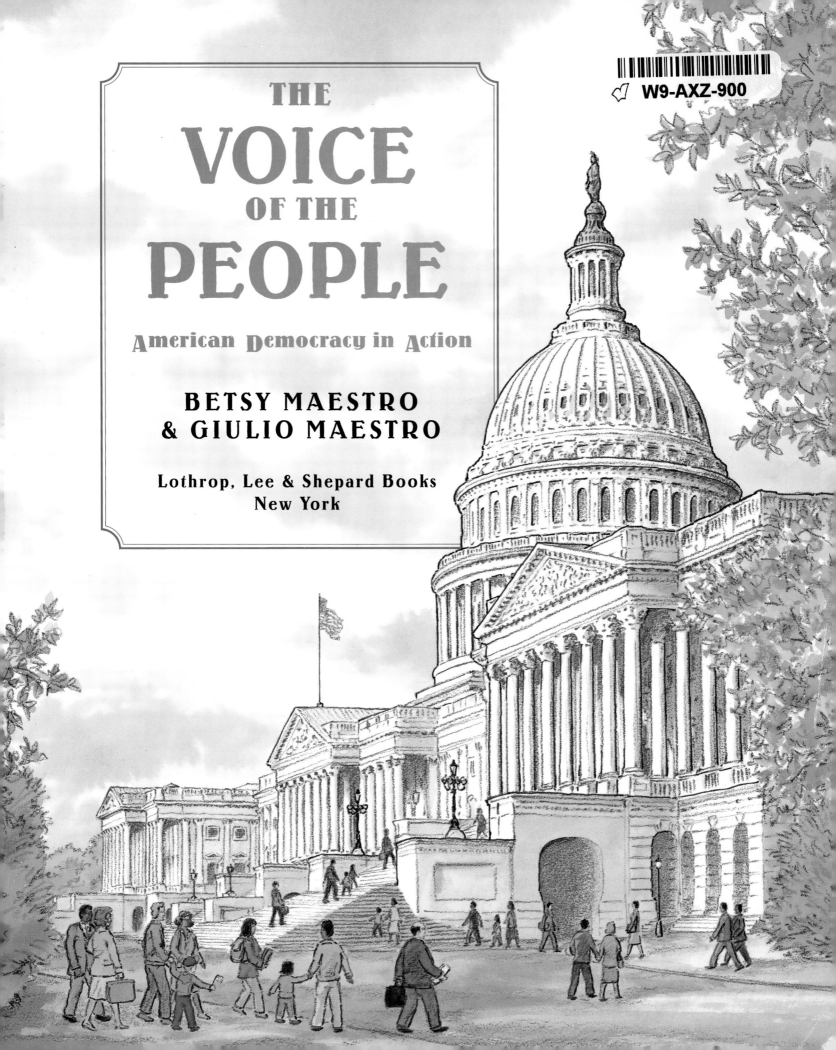

THE VOICE OF THE PEOPLE

American Democracy in Action

BETSY MAESTRO & GIULIO MAESTRO

Lothrop, Lee & Shepard Books
New York

for Chandler Varona-Dixon

Text copyright © 1996 by Betsy C. Maestro; Illustrations copyright © 1996 by Giulio Maestro.
All rights reserved. No part of this book may be reproduced or utilized in any form or by any means, electronic or mechanical, including photocopying and recording, or by any information storage and retrieval system, without permission in writing from the Publisher. Inquiries should be addressed to Lothrop, Lee & Shepard Books, a division of William Morrow & Company, Inc., 1350 Avenue of the Americas, New York, New York 10019.
Manufactured in China
7 8 9 10
Library of Congress Cataloging in Publication Data
Maestro, Betsy. The voice of the people / by Betsy C. Maestro; illustrated by Giulio Maestro.
p.   cm.   Summary: A basic guide to voting and the election process in the United States.
ISBN 0-688-10678-1. — ISBN 0-688-10679-X (lib.bdg.)
1. Voting—United States—Juvenile literature. 2. Elections—United States—Juvenile literature. 3. United States—Politics and government—Juvenile literature. [1. Voting. 2. Elections.] I. Maestro, Giulio, ill. II. Title.
JK1978.M34   1996   324.973—dc20   95-12672 CIP AC

The illustrations in this book were done in watercolor paints and colored pencil. The display type was set in Lo Type.
The text was set in Galliard. Production supervision by Cliff Bryant.

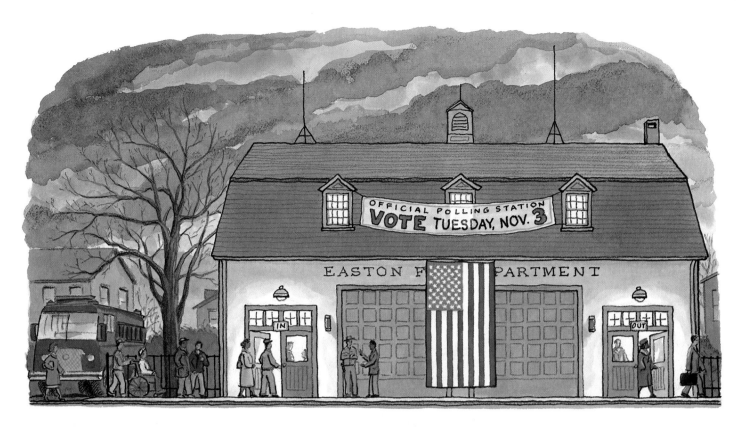

In a small town, people may vote at the firehouse.

I T'S EARLY IN THE MORNING, and people are already lined up at firehouses, schools, and other public buildings all across America. It's Election Day. Throughout this day, people all over the United States will come to these polling places to vote. Every year, on the first or second Tuesday in November, voters have a chance to choose the leaders who will govern their cities and towns, their states, or their country. By voting on Election Day, American citizens participate in their government. They help decide how their cities, states, and country will be run.

CLASS PRESIDENT   SECRETARY

Melanie HHH HHH I   Leon
Jaime   HHH IIII   Sara

VICE PRESIDENT

Samantha HHH III
Trevor   HHH HHH II

Students vote informally for class officers.

Voting is a fair way for groups of people to make decisions. Most people belong to many groups, both small and large, such as families, classes at school, and clubs or organizations. The members of a group must cooperate to get things done. They need leaders and rules. By voting, each person has a voice in deciding the rules and choosing the leaders. The members all agree to follow the choice of the majority, which is more than half of the voting members.

The United States of America is a nation made up of a very large group of people: millions of American citizens. Although they may live thousands of miles apart—from the Atlantic Ocean to the Pacific, from the Gulf of Mexico to the Canadian border, from Alaska to Hawaii—they are all part of this nation. Citizens have rights and privileges, such as free speech and education, and they also have responsibilities—things that they should do for their country. Good citizens obey the country's laws and rules and participate in government by voting on Election Day.

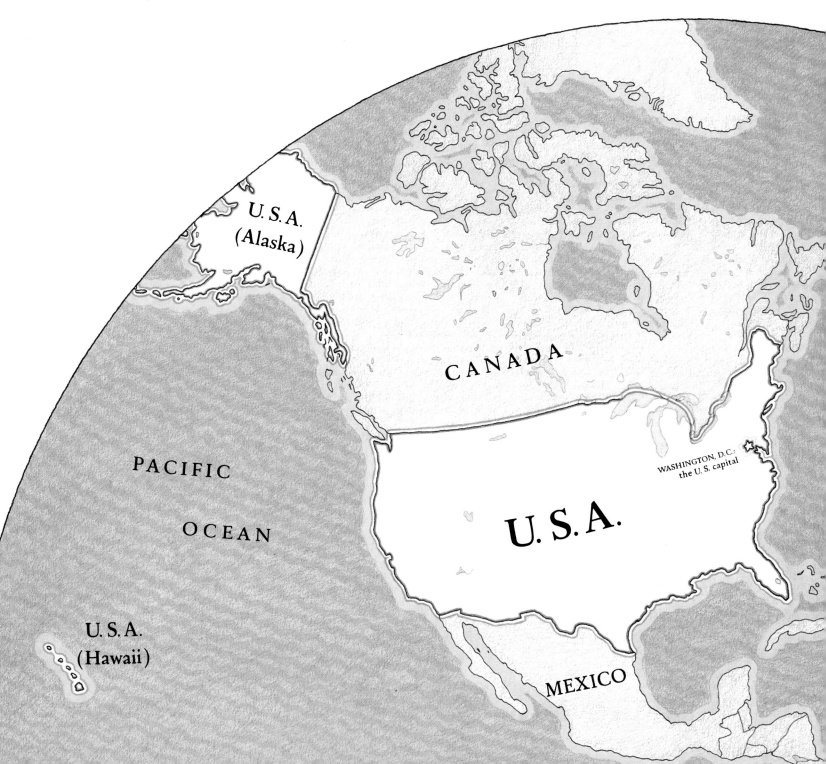

U.S.A.
(Alaska)

CANADA

PACIFIC

OCEAN

WASHINGTON, D.C.:
the U.S. capital

U.S.A.

U.S.A.
(Hawaii)

MEXICO

Every nation has some kind of government—a system for running the country. Not all countries are ruled or run in the same way. Some governments are similar to ours, and others are completely different. Most governments are based on a written set of rules and laws and have a group of officials, or people in charge, with the power to run the country. A government in which the citizens directly participate by voting is called a democracy.

Throughout history, nations have had many different types of government.

Tribal council, North America, 1700s

English Queen, 1500s

Persian King, about 500 B.C.

Greek council, around 200 B.C.

German dictatorship, 1930s

The word democracy comes from two Greek words: *demos,* meaning "people," and *kratos,* meaning "power" or "authority." In a democracy, the power and strength of government come from the people. The United States is a democracy. The word autocracy, the opposite of democracy, comes from the Greek words *autos* ("self") and *kratos* ("power"). It means self-rule or -power. Some countries have autocratic governments: one person or group holds all the power, without the participation— or sometimes even the consent—of the people.

The most important idea in American democracy is that the power of government comes from the people. Most of our ideas about government, laws, and voting come from the Constitution. Over two hundred years ago, when the United States became an independent country, its new leaders had to decide how the young nation would be governed. Men such as George Washington, James Madison, and Benjamin Franklin worked together to make a plan for a new government. More than fifty delegates, from twelve of the original thirteen colonies, met in Philadelphia. Over many months, they wrote the Constitution of the United States. Since that time, American government has been based on the ideas written in that constitution. This important document contains our rules and laws for setting up a government and running the country.

Philadelphia: the State House
(Constitution Hall) in 1799

The writers of our Constitution wanted to make sure that the new nation and its citizens would truly be free and independent. They'd had enough of the autocratic rule of kings and wanted to make sure that the government of the United States would protect the people from a too-powerful government or a too-powerful leader. They wanted to be certain that no part of government, and no leader, could become so strong that the wishes of the people could be denied. So they planned a very special kind of government and then put their plan in writing in the Constitution.

George Washington, James Madison, and Benjamin Franklin at the Constitutional Convention in 1787

The Government of the United States

The Constitution

Executive Branch
The President
The Vice President
The Cabinet

Legislative Branch
The Congress:
Senate
House of Representatives

Judicial Branch
The Supreme Court
lower federal courts

The Constitution describes the powers of the government and the rules it must follow. It provides for three parts or branches of government, each with separate jobs and responsibilities. The legislative branch—the Congress—legislates or makes laws. The executive branch—the President, Vice President, and Cabinet—executes those laws, making sure that they are carried out. This branch also directs and manages the running of government. The judicial branch—or Supreme Court and lower federal courts—settles questions and disagreements about the Constitution and the law. Each branch has some control over the other two, a system known as checks and balances. This ensures that no branch of government becomes too powerful.

The Founding Fathers who wrote the Constitution believed in a federal system of government. In a federal system, the responsibilities of governing are divided between the nation's government and the governments of the states. The powers of the national, or federal, government are listed in the Constitution. Responsibilities not given to the federal government belong to the states. Issues and problems that affect the whole nation are handled by the federal government, which is now based in Washington, D.C., our capital city. State governments, based in the capital cities of each state, deal with more local concerns.

Nebraska State Capitol

Rhode Island State Capitol

Texas State Capitol

Boston in 1790

The authors of our Constitution knew that as the nation grew and changed, the Constitution would need to grow and change as well. In fact, by the time the Constitution was signed by all the states, some changes were already needed. The first changes or additions to the Constitution were called the Bill of Rights. These ten amendments listed some basic freedoms to which all Americans are entitled, such as the right to speak freely and the right to choose one's own religion.

The Bill of Rights

Congress OF THE United States,

begun and held at the City of New York, on
Wednesday, the fourth of March, one thousand seven hundred and eighty nine,

THE Conventions of a number of the States, having at the time of their adopting the Constitution, expressed a desire, in order to prevent misconstruction or abuse of its powers, that further declaratory and restrictive clauses should be added: And as extending the ground of public confidence in the Government, will best ensure the beneficent ends of its institution

RESOLVED by the Senate and House of Representatives of the United States of America in Congress assembled, two thirds of both Houses concurring that the following articles be proposed to the Legislatures of the several States, as amendments to the Constitution of the United States, all, or any of which articles, when ratified by three fourths of the said Legislatures, to be valid to all intents and purposes, as part of the said Constitution, viz.

ARTICLES in addition to, and amendment of the Constitution of the United States of America, proposed by Congress, and ratified by the Legislatures of the several States, pursuant to the fifth article of the original Constitution.

Article the first..... After the first enumeration required by the first article of the Constitution,
one Represent....

Boston in 1990

For over two hundred years, the Constitution has provided the basis and structure for American government. During that time, the country has seen tremendous growth. In 1790, there were barely four million people in the United States. By 1990, the population was almost two hundred fifty million. American government has had to grow and change to keep up with both the population and modern thinking. When the Constitution was first written, women were not allowed to vote. By 1920, times had changed, and women gained the right to vote with the passage of the Nineteenth Amendment. The Constitution still works for the United States, and the strong system of government it created has lasted for more than two centuries.

Women demonstrate for the right to vote in the early 1900s.

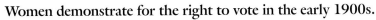

Today the three branches of the federal government provided for in the Constitution—the legislative branch, the executive branch, and the judicial branch—still must work together to make the American system run smoothly.

The United States Capitol: where Congress meets

The Legislature or Congress of the United States is made up of two sections called houses: the Senate and the House of Representatives. The Senate now has one hundred members called Senators, two from each of the fifty states. Each Senator serves a six-year term, or longer if the Senator wins reelection.

The House of Representatives has four hundred thirty-five members. The number of Representatives from each state is determined by population. A state with many people, such as California, may have more than fifty Representatives. States with smaller populations, such as Delaware or Rhode Island, may have only one or two. Although each Representative is elected for a two-year term, many are reelected and serve a number of terms in a row.

The Congress of the United States was given great power and responsibility by the Constitution. Congress is responsible for making new laws and for raising the money needed to run the government. It raises these funds by taxing the American people. Congress also has the power to coin or print money and to declare war on another country. These very important powers are held jointly by both houses of Congress.

Other responsibilities are held by just one house of Congress. Only the Senate can approve treaties or agreements that the President makes with other countries. The Senate must also approve many of the people whom the President chooses for important government jobs.

The House of Representatives is responsible for looking into all matters concerning improper behavior by members of government. In addition, all new laws about raising money and taxes must start in the House.

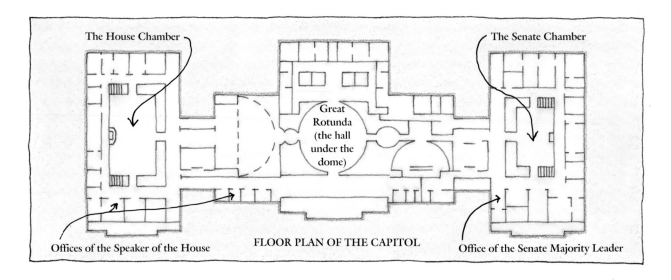

The House Chamber

The Senate Chamber

Great Rotunda (the hall under the dome)

Offices of the Speaker of the House

FLOOR PLAN OF THE CAPITOL

Office of the Senate Majority Leader

The most important job of Congress is to legislate—to make new laws. A plan for a new law is called a bill. Lawmaking or legislating is the process of turning bills into laws. Any of the members of Congress, as well as the President, can begin this process by presenting their bills to Congress. The bills they propose often create new programs that they think the American people need. If the President wants to change the way people are taxed or to start a new health care program, he must first present his ideas to Congress in the form of a bill. Senators and Representatives can also propose bills for new legislation that they think will be good for the country or will help the people in their home states or districts. Sometimes groups of citizens, working together, bring their ideas for new bills to members of Congress, who may assist them by bringing those ideas to the attention of the House or Senate.

When a bill is brought before the Senate or the House, it is sent to a smaller group, called a committee, for study. If the members of the committee feel that the bill has merit—that it is important and deserves to become law—they send it to the full House or the full Senate for a vote. The House or Senate then has a chance to discuss and debate the bill before having to vote yes or no on its passage. If one house of Congress passes the bill, it must next be approved by the other house. If both the Senate and the House of Representatives approve the bill, it is sent to the President for signing. A bill that is not approved is "dead" for that particular session or term of Congress. It may be put aside permanently, or it may be changed somewhat and presented again at a later time.

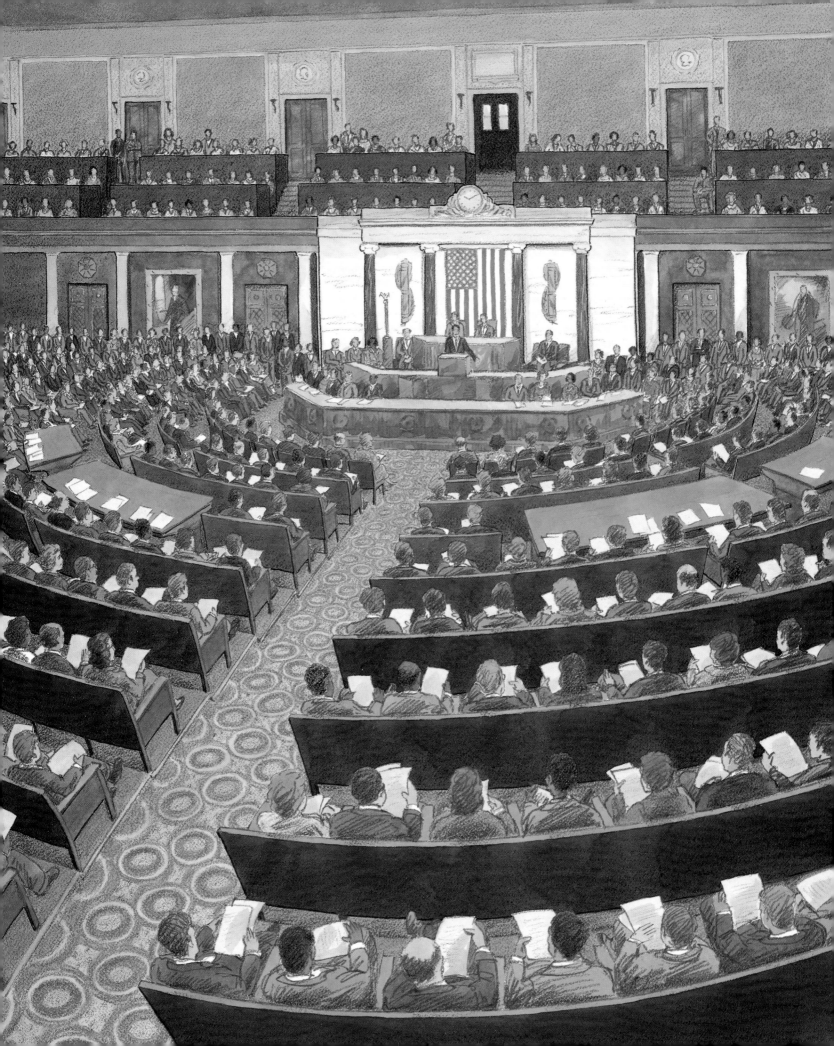

In 1983, President Ronald Reagan signed a bill
making the birthday of Dr. Martin Luther King, Jr., a national holiday.

If the President signs the bill, it becomes law. But the President doesn't always wish to sign the bill. If he is against it, he may choose to say no by vetoing it. Then the bill is sent back to Congress, which can still make it law by a yes vote of two thirds of all the members. When there are not enough votes to override the President, the bill dies. When George Bush was President, for example, Congress tried to override his vetoes thirty-six times but was successful only once. They passed a bill regulating cable television despite a presidential veto. Sometimes a President decides to do nothing: to neither sign nor veto a bill. This may happen if he is not strongly in favor of the bill or strongly against it. In such a case, the bill simply becomes law after ten days without his signature.

Thousands of bills come before Congress in each two-year session. A much smaller number actually become law. In one recent session, almost twelve thousand bills were introduced in Congress. Fewer than five hundred were enacted into law. The creation of a law is a long and difficult process because so many people with different ideas must agree to it. Many changes take place over the many months of discussion and debate, research and study, compromise and rewriting. Senators, Representatives, and the President—more than five hundred people, with differing ideas and views—must cooperate to reach agreement.

Members of Congress have informal discussions
as well as more formal meetings and debates.

Cooperation among the three branches is necessary for American government to work. The executive branch is headed by the President, who is the nation's chief executive. He (or she, when we elect a woman President) is the manager or director of the federal government. The President and Vice President see that the government runs smoothly and that the laws of the land are enforced and obeyed. They must promise to preserve, protect, and defend the Constitution. They serve for a term of four years but may choose to run for one additional term. Only one President, Franklin Delano Roosevelt, was elected more than twice. He won the presidency four times but died shortly into his last term. In 1951, the Twenty-second Amendment to the Constitution was passed, limiting a President to two terms.

The White House:
the President's home and office

President Reagan meeting with his Cabinet

The President relies on many people to help him manage the business of running the executive branch. The members of the Cabinet are among his most important advisers. The President must choose an able leader to head each executive department. The size of the Cabinet has changed over the years. George Washington's first Cabinet had just four Secretaries—one each for the departments of Foreign Affairs (now the Department of State), the Treasury, War (now the Department of Defense), and an Attorney General. The modern Cabinet has fourteen heads of departments as well as a number of other important officials. Some other Cabinet members are the Secretaries of Agriculture, Labor, Health and Human Services, Housing and Urban Development, Transportation, Energy, and Education. The President relies heavily on the Cabinet to help him find solutions for world problems, as well as for domestic issues that directly affect the lives of American citizens.

President Jimmy Carter and Mrs. Carter meet with Egyptian President Sadat *(left)*, and Israeli President Begin *(right)* during peace negotiations at Camp David in 1978.

The President must concern himself with the problems of the world as well as those of the nation. As Chief of State, he acts as the ceremonial head of our government. He travels to other countries to meet with heads of foreign governments, and he greets distinguished visitors to the White House. He works out treaties or agreements with other nations concerning trade and the aid that the United States gives to needy countries. He appoints ambassadors to represent the United States in foreign countries. The President also serves as the Commander in Chief of the armed forces and can send them anywhere in the world to protect our interests or to keep the peace in troubled places.

President Richard Nixon visits American troops in South Vietnam in 1969.

President Bill Clinton throws out the first baseball of the season.

A President has so many important tasks that there is little time for rest or leisure. But he finds time for some very enjoyable duties, such as lighting the White House Christmas tree, throwing the first ball to open the baseball season, rolling eggs on the lawn at Easter, and entertaining at the White House.

The writers of the Constitution intended Congress to be the most powerful branch of government. Today the President's power is about equal to that of Congress; but although he is the single most important figure in our government, he must still have congressional approval for many of his actions. He must report on the State of the Union at the beginning of each session of Congress. In this important speech, the President gives his opinion of how the country is doing and presents his ideas about what needs to be done in the coming years. He follows up by sending his proposals for programs and legislation to Congress for consideration. When the President and Congress cooperate, the work of government moves along smoothly. When they do not, very little can be accomplished.

The judicial branch of government (the Supreme Court and lower federal courts) works independently of the other two branches. The Supreme Court is the highest court in the land and has a Chief Justice or head judge and eight Associate Justices. Once they are appointed by the President and approved by a vote of the Senate, the Justices serve for life unless they choose to retire. More than one hundred Justices have served on the Court since our government was established, and until recently all were men. The first woman named to the Supreme Court was Sandra Day O'Connor, who was appointed in 1981. A second woman, Ruth Bader Ginsburg, was seated in 1993.

The Supreme Court in 1995. *Behind table from left:* Clarence Thomas, Antonin Scalia, William Rehnquist, Sandra Day O'Connor, Anthony Kennedy, David Souter, and Ruth Bader Ginsburg.
Seated in front: John Paul Stevens *(left)* and Stephen Breyer *(right)*.

The motto of the Supreme Court is "Equal Justice under Law." The Supreme Court explains and interprets the Constitution when questions concerning particular laws arise in lower courts. It alone can decide whether or not laws are constitutional—whether they are in keeping with the ideals of our Constitution. The Justices make careful decisions based on the principles of the Constitution and the arguments presented before them. They should not be swayed in their rulings by public opinion or by their own attitudes or beliefs. While the decisions and judgments reached in lower courts may be appealed or questioned, the decisions of the Supreme Court are absolute and final. Although thousands of requests for rulings reach the Supreme Court each year, fewer than one hundred fifty are actually considered and ruled upon.

The Supreme Court Building

Every year, thousands of lawyers from all over the country go to the Supreme Court hoping to plead their cases. But the Supreme Court rules only on the most important cases—most often, those that concern basic freedoms and civil rights that are protected by the Bill of Rights. The Justices settle disputes between states and between states and the federal government. The Court can also decide whether someone has received a fair trial in a lower court.

Sometimes the Supreme Court is asked to make a decision so important that the whole country pays careful attention to its ruling. In 1954, the Court ruled that racial segregation—the separation of black and white people—in public schools was unconstitutional. Chief Justice Earl Warren wrote the Court's unanimous opinion outlawing that kind of separation in public schools. This decision affected schools all over the United States and paved the way for new civil rights laws passed in the years that followed.

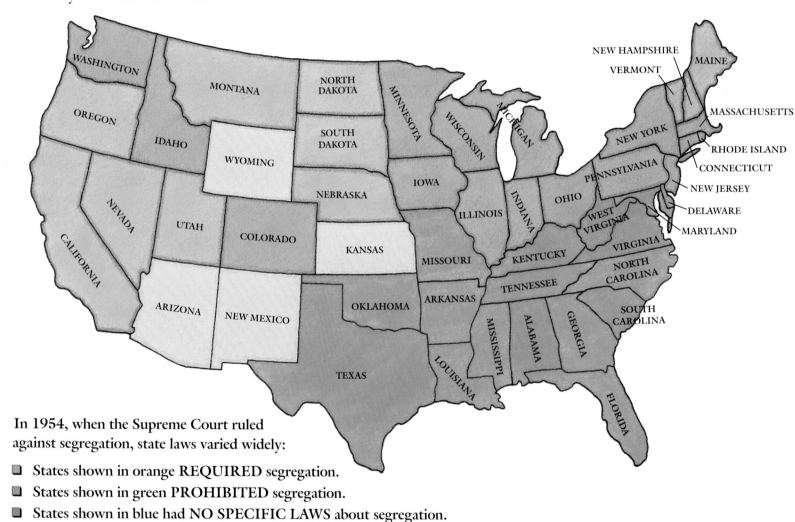

In 1954, when the Supreme Court ruled against segregation, state laws varied widely:

❑ States shown in orange **REQUIRED** segregation.
❑ States shown in green **PROHIBITED** segregation.
❑ States shown in blue had **NO SPECIFIC LAWS** about segregation.
❑ States shown in yellow made segregation a **LOCAL OPTION**.

Above: When integration was ordered by the Supreme Court, National Guard troops were needed to protect the right of African-American students to attend school in Little Rock, Arkansas.

Below: As late as 1963, police in some southern states still interfered with the freedom of civil rights demonstrators, using dogs and fire hoses to disperse them.

In a democracy, citizens choose the people who will serve in government. The Constitution outlines the process for electing members of the federal government. Most of the rules and laws of our election system are included in the document itself or in amendments added over the years. Other parts of the election process have developed from American customs and traditions. Government may sometimes seem distant or separate from the people, but all citizens over the age of eighteen have the right and responsibility to help choose the national leaders who will represent them in Washington.

Buttons like this were worn by young people before the passage of the 26th amendment to the Constitution. When signed into law on July 5, 1971, it lowered the voting age from 21 to 18.

U.S. Constitution
AMENDMENT 26
Administrator of General Services

Certification of Amendment to Constitution of the United States Extending the Right to Vote to Citizens Eighteen Years of Age or Older

To All to Whom These Presents Shall Come, Greeting:

KNOW YE, That the Congress of the United States, at the first session, Ninety-second Congress begun at the City of Washington on Thursday, the twenty-first day of January, in the year one thousand nine hundred and seventy-one, passed a Joint Resolution in the words and figures as follows: to wit—

JOINT RESOLUTION

Proposing an amendment to the Constitution of the United States extending the right to vote to citizens eighteen years of age or older.

Resolved by the Senate and House of Representatives of the United States of America in Congress assembled (two-thirds of each House concurring therein), That the following article is proposed as an amendment to the Constitution of the United States, which shall be valid to all intents and purposes as part of the Constitution when ratified by the legislatures of three-fourths of the several States within seven years from the date of its submission by the Congress:

"Article—

"SECTION 1. The right of citizens of the United States, who are eighteen years of age or older, to vote shall not be denied or abridged by the United States or by any State on account of age.

"SEC. 2. The Congress shall have power to enforce this article by appropriate legislation."

And, further, that it appears from official d

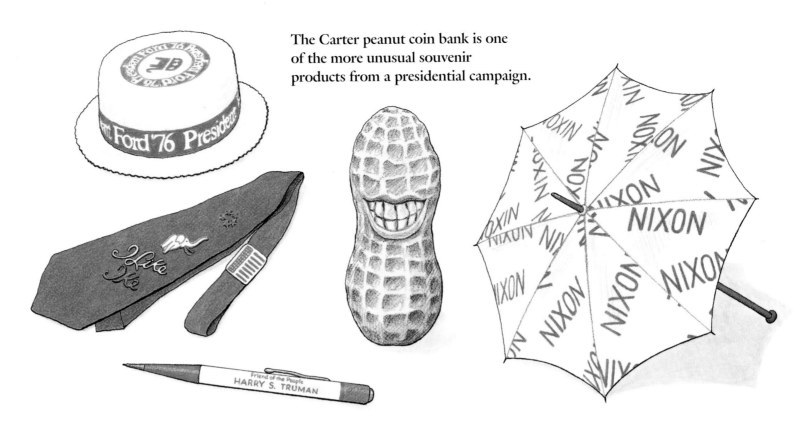

The Carter peanut coin bank is one of the more unusual souvenir products from a presidential campaign.

The election of the President, which is held every four years, is one of the most important events in American government and politics. It is often compared to a race: We say that someone is "running for office" and that the "presidential race" is on. People who are trying to be elected to a particular official job are called candidates. Almost any citizen who wants to be President can announce that he or she is a candidate. Most often, however, candidates for President are people with a lot of experience in government, such as Governors of states or members of Congress. The process of choosing presidential candidates begins more than a year before the actual election.

Supporters of the different candidates for President and Vice President often wear campaign buttons.

People gather at a political rally for presidential candidate Gerald Ford.

Candidates for public office want to make sure that many Americans know about them and are familiar with their ideas. Presidential candidates try to travel to all fifty states, while candidates for other offices may campaign only in their own states or cities. Candidates want everyone to recognize their names and faces. Some are already well known to the American public. Bill Bradley of New Jersey was a basketball star and John Glenn of Ohio was an astronaut before they became Senators. Ronald Reagan was a movie actor before serving as Governor of California and later as President of the United States.

Candidates shake hands, greet people, give speeches, and kiss babies. They appear on TV and radio shows, run ads in newspapers, and argue with other candidates during televised debates. Presidential candidates want the voters to know what they stand for—their ideas on important issues and problems. They talk about what they will do if they win the race for President.

Each candidate usually belongs to one particular political party—a group of people with similar ideas about government. There are two main political parties in the United States: the Democratic party and the Republican party. There are some smaller parties as well, so more than two candidates often run for President. In 1992, Ross Perot ran for President as a third-party candidate against Democrat Bill Clinton and Republican George Bush.

Although there may be many candidates to begin with, only one from each party will eventually be chosen to run for President. Months before the actual presidential election, people who are members of the two main political parties often help to select that one person by voting in primary elections that are held in many states.

Newspapers keep voters informed of how the candidates are doing.

The primary election season usually begins in February in the snows of New Hampshire and ends early in June. On Super Tuesday in March, more than seven states hold their presidential primaries all on the same day. In each state primary, party members from that state choose the candidate they prefer. In some states, candidates are chosen at a large state meeting called a convention, or at smaller meetings called caucuses.

Primary day in New Hampshire

All of the states participate in the huge national conventions held by the Democrats and Republicans every four years. These gatherings take place in the summer before the presidential election. Each state party sends delegates, representing the state's voters, to vote for the candidate or candidates preferred in their state.

Delegates arrive at a big city convention hall.

When the conventions end, each party will have its final candidate for President and Vice President. At the conventions, each party also writes its platform: a plan of action for the government in the next four years. The platform lists the ideas that the party will "stand" on. It outlines the party position on the important problems that face the nation. The platform may propose solutions for these problems.

When Abraham Lincoln was a candidate, slavery was the biggest issue. In the 1960s and 1970s, the Vietnam War was on everyone's mind. More recently, candidates and parties have had to show where they stand on health-care reform, the economy and budget, and the environment.

At the national convention, everyone gathers in a huge hall to choose the party's candidate for President. Each of the fifty states has sent a delegation, a group of people, to represent its voters. States with large populations have many delegates, while smaller states may have only a few. During the roll call of the states, the names of all the candidates are placed in nomination to be considered by the entire convention. When each state is called again, the delegates cast their votes for the candidates who are most popular in their states.

The 1980 Republican National Convention

Sometimes one candidate has enough votes to be declared the winner after just one ballot or roll-call vote. Other times no one has a clear majority, and there must be another call of the roll. Some delegates may now change their votes. Balloting continues until there is a winner. In 1924, it took the Democrats fourteen days and over one hundred ballots to select a candidate! Luckily, this was a very unusual occurrence. The candidate who is the winner—the one with the most votes— becomes the party's choice for President of the United States.

Before 1932, candidates didn't go to the conventions. But in that year, Franklin Delano Roosevelt flew to Chicago to accept the Democratic nomination in person. Since then, it has been part of American political tradition for the candidate to make a personal appearance at the convention.

Near the close of the convention, a vice presidential candidate is chosen. The candidate for President and the party leaders give a great deal of thought to selecting a running mate. The party wants to have a "balanced ticket"—two candidates who come from different backgrounds. One may be from the East, the other from the West or South. One candidate may have been a Governor, the other a Senator. One may come from a wealthy family, while the other candidate may be from a poor one. They may practice different religions. Such differences help create a very broad appeal, so that many voters will feel they have something in common with one or both of the candidates.

When the speeches and celebrations are over, the convention closes and almost everyone goes home. For the candidates, though, the really hard work is just beginning. After the major parties choose their candidates, the final campaign gets under way. For the next few months, the race for the White House is front-page news. Almost everyone in the country is thinking about the campaign. The candidates go out on the road again, meeting the voters. They give hundreds, if not thousands, of speeches. During debates on nationwide television, the candidates answer questions and discuss and argue their ideas with one another. They are interviewed by radio, TV, and newspaper reporters, and pictures of the candidates appear in most newspapers and magazines. Their names become household words—everyone in the United States of America recognizes them.

In 1960, John F. Kennnedy and Richard M. Nixon were the first presidential candidates to debate on nationwide television.

A voting machine has a lever to push down for each candidate the voter selects.

OFFICES ▶	1 Presidential Electors for	2 United States Senator	3 Representative in Congress	4 State Senator	5 State Representative	6 Registrar of Voters	7
A CONNECTICUT PARTY	1A	2A Christopher J. Dodd	3A Sam Gejdenson	4A Melodie Peters	5A Gary Orefice	6A	7A
REPUBLICAN	1B Bush and Quayle	2B Brook Johnson	3B Edward W. Munster	4B Robert S. Tuneski	5B Frederick Lundfelt	6B Judith Tooker Kerr	7B
DEMOCRATIC	1C Clinton and Gore	2C Christopher J. Dodd	3C Sam Gejdenson	4C Melodie Peters	5C Gary Orefice	6C Patricia M. McCarthy	7C
CONCERNED CITIZENS	1D	2D Richard D. Gregory	3D	4D	5D	6D	7D
AMERICANS FOR PEROT	1E Perot and Stockdale	2E	3E	4E	5E	6E	7E

By the time November comes, almost everyone is glad that the campaigns are ending. It has been an exhausting year for the candidates and all their workers. Election Day is the first Tuesday after the first Monday in November. People all over the United States of America go to polling places in their neighborhoods to vote. Most use electronic voting machines, but some mark paper ballots to choose the candidate they want for President of the United States. From early in the morning to late in the evening, from Maine to Hawaii, from Florida to Alaska, voters cast their ballots. When all the votes are counted, the nation will know who the next President will be.

Reporters question voters as they leave polling places around the country. The information they gather, along with early electronic results from voting machines, enables the television networks to predict winners even before all the polls close. Toward the end of the evening, a winner is announced based on the popular vote—the vote of the people. Then the President-elect makes a victory speech. Even the losing candidate has to give one more speech to congratulate the winner and to thank all those who helped with the campaign.

Facing page: **People voting at a big city public school on Election Day**

Before a new President takes office, the members of the Electoral College must meet and vote. Most Americans find this part of the election process difficult to understand. Long ago, when the Constitution was written, there were no strong political parties to help select candidates, and average citizens could neither read nor write. The leaders of the new country worried about what kind of President the people might choose and were afraid to let them vote for the President directly. Instead, they worked out a system in which the citizens would vote for electors rather than for the actual candidates. These electors were men who were well educated and knew something about government, and the Founding Fathers trusted them to elect a good President.

Even now, when Americans vote in presidential elections, they actually choose electors pledged to particular candidates. In December, these electors go to their state capitals to cast votes for the candidates they represent. The candidate with the most votes in each state gets all the electoral votes of that state.

In Washington, D.C., at a joint session of Congress in January, the electoral votes of all the states are counted. The candidate with the majority of electoral votes is now officially declared President-elect. The number of electoral votes is based on a state's population. California has fifty-four; Texas, thirty-two; Vermont and Delaware, only three each. In all, there are five hundred thirty-eight votes and the winner must have at least two hundred seventy. The popular vote, numbered in the millions, is the actual number of votes cast by the people. But it is the electoral vote that officially elects the President.

Facing Page: This chart shows the popular and electoral vote totals, state by state, for the 1992 presidential election. The final electoral vote totals were 370 for Clinton (in blue), 168 for Bush, and 0 for Perot; 270 electoral votes are needed to win. Perot received no electoral votes because he did not win the popular vote in any state.

THE 1992 PRESIDENTIAL ELECTION

State	Electoral votes	(Republican) George Bush Dan Quayle Popular vote	(Democrat) Bill Clinton Albert Gore Popular vote	(Independent) Ross Perot James Stockdale Popular vote
Alabama	9	797,477	686,146	180,209
Alaska	3	81,875	63,498	55,085
Arizona	8	548,148	525,031	341,148
Arkansas	6	333,487	497,875	98,100
California	54	3,338,942	4,812,317	2,144,856
Colorado	8	557,706	626,207	362,813
Connecticut	8	574,738	681,091	348,028
Delaware	3	102,436	125,997	59,061
District of Columbia	3	19,813	186,301	9,284
Florida	25	2,137,752	2,051,845	1,041,607
Georgia	13	988,530	1,005,564	307,326
Hawaii	4	136,430	178,893	52,863
Idaho	4	201,787	136,249	129,897
Illinois	22	1,718,178	2,379,486	832,462
Indiana	12	970,457	829,176	448,431
Iowa	7	503,004	583,513	251,725
Kansas	6	444,571	386,816	311,449
Kentucky	8	616,517	664,246	203,682
Louisana	9	729,880	815,305	210,604
Maine	4	207,122	261,859	205,076
Maryland	10	671,609	941,979	271,198
Massachusetts	12	804,534	1,315,016	630,440
Michigan	18	1,587,105	1,858,275	820,855
Minnesota	10	737,281	996,919	551,167
Mississippi	7	481,583	392,929	84,496
Missouri	11	811,057	1,053,040	518,250
Montana	3	143,702	153,899	106,869
Nebraska	5	339,108	214,064	172,043
Nevada	4	171,378	185,401	129,532
New Hampshire	4	199,623	207,264	120,029
New Jersey	15	1,309,724	1,366,609	505,698
New Mexico	5	211,442	258,429	91,204
New York	33	2,241,283	3,246,787	1,029,038
North Carolina	14	1,122,608	1,103,716	353,845
North Dakota	3	135,441	98,917	70,759
Ohio	21	1,876,445	1,965,204	1,024,598
Oklahoma	8	592,929	473,066	319,978
Oregon	7	394,356	525,123	307,860
Pennsylvania	23	1,779,699	2,226,006	896,788
Rhode Island	4	121,916	198,924	94,757
South Carolina	8	572,614	476,304	138,018
South Dakota	3	136,671	124,861	73,297
Tennessee	11	840,899	933,520	199,787
Texas	32	2,459,921	2,278,688	1,349,627
Utah	5	320,559	182,850	202,605
Vermont	3	85,512	125,803	61,510
Virginia	13	1,147,226	1,034,781	344,852
Washington	11	609,912	855,710	470,239
West Virginia	5	239,103	326,936	106,367
Wisconsin	11	926,245	1,035,943	542,660
Wyoming	3	79,558	67,863	51,209

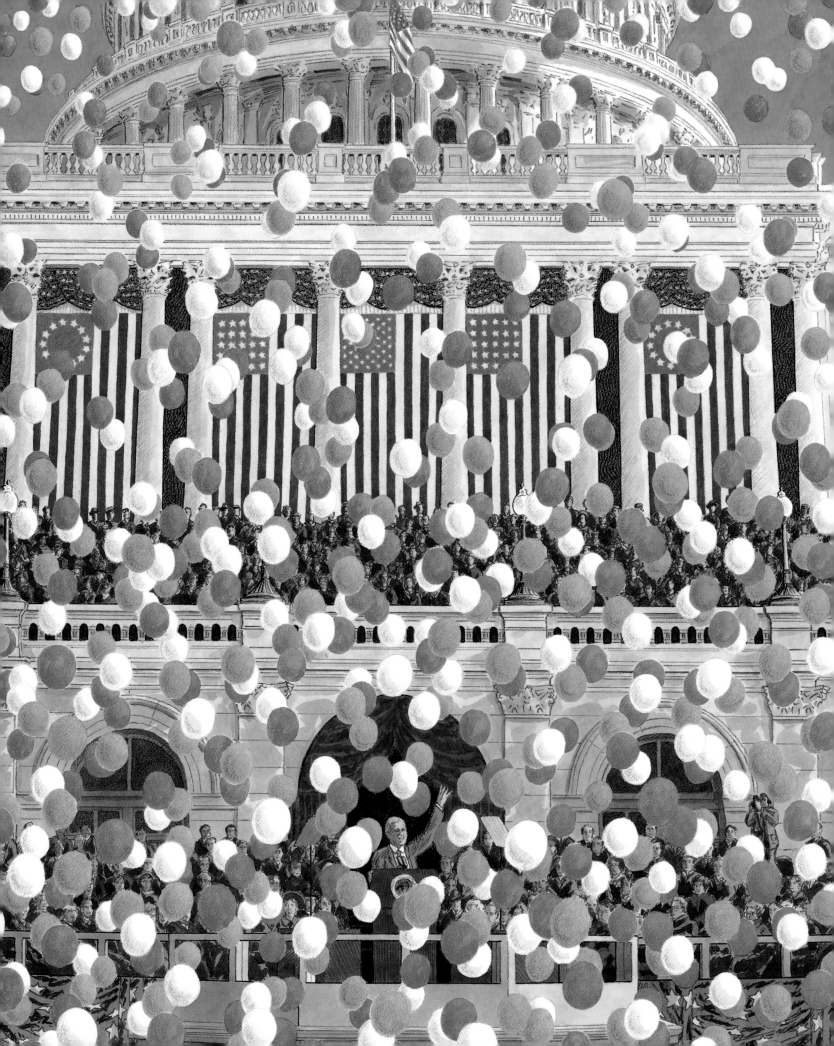

Between November and January, when the President-elect takes office, there is a lot to be done. When a current President has been reelected, the work of government goes on, exactly as before, with no changes in the executive branch. However, when a new President has been elected, he or she must very quickly learn about the job of being President. The President-elect and the current President may meet many times during this short transition period.

On January 20, the new President is inaugurated. A reelected President must be sworn in again. Outside the Capitol Building, the Chief Justice of the Supreme Court reads the Oath of Office. The President and Vice President swear to be faithful to the Constitution and to do their jobs to the best of their abilities. After the official ceremony, there is a huge parade up Pennsylvania Avenue to the White House. The new President rides in a limousine or walks along the parade route, waving to the crowds. At night, many fancy inaugural balls are held all over the city of Washington to celebrate the President's election.

All our elected officials, from President to Mayor, are elected in a similar process. Except for the President, however, they are all elected directly by the people, without the help of the Electoral College. American government depends on this process of participation and choice. This is what our Constitution established and what our democracy is all about. As each citizen turns eighteen, he or she gains the right and the responsibility to vote. Each citizen holds in his or her hands a tiny bit of the power of our government. Together, the millions of citizens across the United States join to help our country and our government of the people, by the people, and for the people move forward, ever stronger.

Facing page: **Bill Clinton waves to well-wishers at his inauguration as the 42nd President of the United States of America on January 20, 1993.**

Additional Information
About Our Constitution and Government

The Constitution of the United States
PREAMBLE

We the People of the United States, in Order to form a more perfect Union,
establish Justice, insure domestic Tranquility, provide for the common defence,
promote the general Welfare, and secure the Blessings of Liberty to ourselves
and our Posterity, do ordain and establish this Constitution for
the United States of America.

Article I

Lists rules for forming and running Congress, the lawmaking branch of government. Divides Congress into two houses, the Senate and the House of Representatives, and sets out the duties of each house. Lists the powers of the federal government.

Article II

Calls for a President to carry out the nation's laws. Describes procedures for electing the President and lists the President's powers.

Article III

Establishes a Supreme Court. Defines, and sets out laws dealing with, treason against the United States.

Article IV

Forbids any state from treating a citizen of another state differently from its own citizens. Gives Congress the power to admit new states to the Union.

Article V

Lists steps for amending (adding to or changing) the Constitution. Changes approved by at least three-fourths of the states become law.

Article VI

Makes the new Constitution the supreme law of the land and requires all federal and state officials to support it.

Article VII

Establishes that if at least nine states ratify the Constitution of 1787, it is considered the law of the land.

Summary of the Amendments to the Constitution

The first ten amendments make up the Bill of Rights, adopted in 1791.

Amendment I Guarantees freedom of religion, of speech, and of the press. Gives the people the right to meet peaceably and the right to voice complaints to the government.

Amendment II Guarantees the right to keep and bear arms.

Amendment III Sets conditions for housing soldiers in peacetime and in wartime.

Amendment IV Guarantees the right to privacy. Limits the power of government to search and seize property.

Amendment V Establishes trial procedures. Forbids punishment without a trial. Guarantees compensation if property is taken by the government for public use.

Amendment VI Guarantees the right to a speedy, fair trial by jury in criminal cases.

Amendment VII Provides for a jury trial in civil lawsuits exceeding the value of twenty dollars.

Amendment VIII Prohibits excessive bail and fines, and cruel and unusual punishment.

Amendment IX Establishes that the people hold more rights than only those listed in the Constitution.

Amendment X Declares that powers not given by the Constitution to the central goverment, or forbidden to the states, are reserved for the states or the people.

XI (1798) Keeps any one of the states from being sued by citizens of another state or of a foreign country.

XII (1804) Sets presidential election procedures.

XIII (1865) Abolishes slavery.

XIV (1868) Forbids laws that unfairly deny citizens' rights and guarantees equal protection under the law to all.

XV (1870) Forbids depriving citizens of the right to vote because of their race or color.

XVI (1913) Authorizes an income tax.

XVII (1913) Calls for Senators to be elected by direct vote of the people.

XVIII (1919) The Prohibition Amendment. Forbids the manufacture or sale of liquor.

XIX (1920) Grants women the right to vote.

XX (1933) Starts presidential and congressional terms in January.

XXI (1933) Repeals the Eighteenth Amendment.

XXII (1951) Bars any President from serving more than ten years.

XXIII (1961) Gives residents of the District of Columbia (Washington, D.C.) the right to vote for President.

XXIV (1964) Outlaws the payment of taxes as a voting requirement.

XXV (1967) Sets up rules for succession if a President cannot complete the term.

XXVI (1971) Lowers the legal voting age to eighteen.

XXVII (1992) Prohibits any law that changes the salaries of Senators and Representatives from taking effect until after the next election of the House of Representatives.

UNITED STATES PRESIDENTS

George Washington 1789-1797
John Adams 1797-1801
Thomas Jefferson 1801-1809
James Madison 1809-1817
James Monroe 1817-1825
John Quincy Adams 1825-1829
Andrew Jackson 1829-1837
Martin Van Buren 1837-1841
William Henry Harrison 1841*
John Tyler 1841-1845
James K. Polk 1845-1849
Zachary Taylor 1849-1850*
Millard Fillmore 1850-1853
Franklin Pierce 1853-1857
James Buchanan 1857-1861
Abraham Lincoln 1861-1865**
Andrew Johnson 1865-1869
Ulysses S. Grant 1869-1877
Rutherford B. Hayes 1877-1881
James A. Garfield 1881**
Chester B. Arthur 1881-1885

Grover Cleveland 1885-1889
Benjamin Harrison 1889-1893
Grover Cleveland 1893-1897
William McKinley 1897-1901**
Theodore Roosevelt 1901-1909
William Howard Taft 1909-1913
Woodrow Wilson 1913-1921
Warren G. Harding 1921-1923*
Calvin Coolidge 1923-1929
Herbert Hoover 1929-1933
Franklin D. Roosevelt 1933-1945*
Harry S. Truman 1945-1953
Dwight D. Eisenhower 1953-1961
John F. Kennedy 1961-1963**
Lyndon B. Johnson 1963-1969
Richard M. Nixon 1969-1974***
Gerald R. Ford 1974-1977
Jimmy Carter 1977-1981
Ronald Reagan 1981-1989
George Bush 1989-1993
Bill Clinton 1993-

*died in office   **killed in office   ***resigned

Order of Presidential Succession

If a President dies in office, then the Vice President becomes President. If both should die, the Presidency passes to the Speaker of the House of Representatives. Then, the order of succession is as follows:
President pro tempore of the
   Senate
Secretary of State
Secretary of the Treasury
Secretary of Defense
Attorney General
Other Cabinet members follow

The Oath of Office

The President and Vice President take the following oath when they are inaugurated:

"I do solemnly swear (or affirm) that I will faithfully execute the office of President [or Vice President] of the United States, and will to the best of my ability, preserve, protect and defend the Constitution of the United States."

The President's Salary

The United States of America has had forty-two Presidents. The first seventeen Presidents earned a yearly salary of $25,000. In 1873, it was doubled to $50,000. It was increased to $75,000 in 1909, and to $100,000 in 1949. The President's salary was raised to $200,000 in 1969. In addition to salary, the President receives living and travel expenses.

A HOME FOR THE CONSTITUTION

The original Constitution of the United States is kept under guard in the Exhibition Hall of the National Archives Building in Washington, D.C. Many other important national documents are also stored there, including the Declaration of Independence. Each year, thousands of visitors come to see these documents. Sealed cases made of bronze and glass hold these two special documents. The cases contain the gas helium, which prevents moisture and dust from damaging the papers. Tinted glass protects the documents from light. In case of a fire or explosion, the cases would automatically be lowered into a fireproof and bombproof vault located twenty feet below the floor.

OTHER GOVERNMENT ELECTIONS

Although presidential elections occur only every four years, voters choose some government officials every year on Election Day. Congressional elections are held every two years, for the entire House of Representatives and one-third of the Senate. In other years, there are elections for state and local government officials. A Governor is at the head of each state government. State governments are often similar in structure to the federal government. There are state Senators and Representatives to be elected. City and town governments usually have a Mayor or First Selectperson as their chief executives. A big city may have a government of thousands of people. A small town sometimes has only a few people in its government.

MORE ABOUT THE ELECTORAL COLLEGE

To win the popular vote, a presidential candidate does not have to have a majority, or more than half of the votes cast. The winner of the popular vote simply has more votes than the other candidates. To win the electoral vote, a presidential candidate must have a majority, which means getting more than half of the 538 electoral votes. The candidate must have at least 270 electoral votes to become President. The winner of the electoral majority is nearly always the person who won the popular vote on election night. Only three times in American history, in 1824, 1876, and 1888, has a President been elected who was not the winner of the popular vote. This can happen if no candidate has a majority of electoral votes and the election has to be decided by the House of Representatives. It can also happen when the popular vote is very close and one candidate has won in more states with large numbers of electoral votes.

OTHER INTERESTING FACTS

James Madison is known as the "Father of the Constitution." His belief in the importance of a strong central government was influential in shaping the Constitution.

George Washington was the only President who did not live in the White House—it wasn't built yet. The first President's House was occupied in 1800. This residence was burned by the British in 1814 (in the War of 1812). The new residence was completed in 1817 but was not officially called the White House until 1902.

Our federal government employs more than two million workers.

In the early days of government, Congress searched for an appropriate title for the President. They considered titles such as "His Elective Majesty," but finally settled on a simple "Mr. President."

The first Congress met in 1789 in New York City. A few years later, it moved to Philadelphia. It met in Washington, D.C., for the first time in 1800.

In September 1960, about sixty million viewers tuned in to watch the first presidential election debate carried live on television. The two candidates were Vice President Richard Nixon and Senator John Kennedy.

No other presidential candidate ran against George Washington. He ran unopposed in 1789 and in 1792.

In 1910, William Howard Taft became the first President to throw the first pitch in a baseball game. The Washington Senators were playing the Philadelphia Athletics.

Special-interest groups and industries spend millions of dollars every year attempting to influence members of Congress to vote their way. Their paid representatives are called lobbyists.

Many Presidents have had interesting nicknames. Andrew Jackson was known as "Old Hickory" because he was thought to be as tough as hickory wood. Zachary Taylor was called "Old Rough and Ready" because of his long and distinguished military career.

The wives of our male Presidents are known as First Ladies. Some, like Dolley Madison, were known as great hostesses. Eleanor Roosevelt and others took an active role in the affairs of the country. No one knows what we will call the husband of the first female President.

The White House has 132 rooms, including a movie theater, a gym, and a barbershop. The first President's House had only six rooms. The White House had running water installed in 1833. Telephone service began in 1877, and electricity was installed in 1891.

In December, following presidential elections, sealed lists of the electors' votes from each state are mailed to the President of the Senate. On January 6, he opens them in front of a joint session of Congress and the electoral votes of all the states are counted.